ESSEX-HUDSON
BOOK EVALUATION

BUFFALO GIRLS

for Sarah, Katie, and Bill

A Lucas/Evans Book

Copyright © 1987 by Bobette McCarthy
Published by Crown Publishers, Inc., 225 Park Avenue South, New York,
New York 10003 and represented in Canada by the Canadian MANDA Group.
CROWN is a trademark of Crown Publishers, Inc.
Manufactured in Japan
Library of Congress Cataloging-in-Publication Data. McCarthy, Bobette. Buffalo girls.
"A Lucas/Evans book."
Summary: An illustrated version of the traditional folk song, in which the buffalo girls
sing by starlight and dance by the light of the moon.
1. Folk-songs, American—Texts. [1. Folk songs, American] I. Title. PZ8.3.M128Bu
1987   784.4'05   86-29069
ISBN 0-517-56568-4

10 9 8 7 6 5 4 3 2 1

First Edition

Buffalo Girls

Bobette McCarthy

Crown Publishers, Inc.
New York

Buffalo Girls, won't you come out tonight,
come out tonight, come out tonight?

Buffalo Girls, won't you come out tonight
and dance by the light of the moon?

Buffalo Girls have lots of fun.
They like to swim in the lake

or bask in the sun.

They dance the Hoochie Coochie
when work is done.
They dance by the light of the moon!

Buffalo Girls are plenty smart.
They like to put things together
and take things apart.

They can make a covered wagon
or an apple tart, and they can dance
by the light of the moon.

Buffalo Girls are not genteel.

They love to holler,
but they never squeal.

There is nothing they like better
than a good hot meal.

And they dance by the light of the moon.

"Come and feel the magic,
come and heed the call..."
croon the Buffalo Boys
from the Buffalo Hall.
"We can sing by starlight
and that's not all."

"We can dance by the light of the moon."

Oh will you, won't you, will you, won't you

come out tonight, come out tonight?

Oh, Buffalo Girls, won't you
come out tonight

and dance by the light of the moon!

BUFFALO GIRLS

Buf-fa-lo Girls won't you come out to-night,

come out to-night, come out to-night?

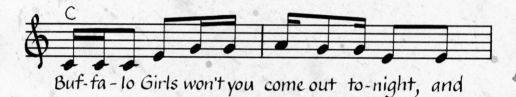

Buf-fa-lo Girls won't you come out to-night, and

dance by the light of the moon?

The song that has come to be known as "Buffalo Girls" is descended from a tune written in 1844 by a minstrel named Cool White. White's song enjoyed great popularity with traveling shows. Performers improvised and rewrote the verses of many songs to suit their needs. (Hence the song became Buffalo Gals when playing Buffalo, Philly Gals when playing Philadelphia, etc.) Following the tradition of the traveling performers, I had enormous fun reworking, and embellishing, the verses for this picture book. —B. McCarthy

DATE DUE

AUG 1 3 2004	
AUG 1 6 2004	
AUG 1 8 2004	

DEMCO, INC. 38-2931